COMPASS
True Stories for Kids

There be Pirates!

Swashbucklers & Rogues of the Atlantic

Joann Hamilton-Barry

NIMBUS
PUBLISHING

Nimbus Publishing Limited
3660 Strawberry Hill St, Halifax, NS B3K 5A9
(902) 455-4286 nimbus.ca

Printed and bound in Canada

NB1300

Design: Andrew Herygers
Library and Archives Canada Cataloguing in Publication

Hamilton-Barry, Joann, author
There be pirates! : swashbucklers & rogues of the Atlantic / Joann Hamilton-Barry.
(Compass series)
Issued in print and electronic formats.
ISBN 978-1-77108-579-3 (softcover).—ISBN 978-1-77108-580-9 (HTML)

1. Pirates—Atlantic Coast (Canada)—History—Juvenile literature.
2. Piracy—Atlantic Coast (Canada)—History—Juvenile literature.
3. Atlantic Coast (Canada)—History—Juvenile literature.
I. Title. II. Series: Compass (Halifax, N.S.)

FC2346.4.L39 2017   j971.6'22503   C2017-904097-9

Nimbus Publishing acknowledges the financial support for its publishing activities from the Government of Canada, the Canada Council for the Arts, and from the Province of Nova Scotia. We are pleased to work in partnership with the Province of Nova Scotia to develop and promote our creative industries for the benefit of all Nova Scotians.

To my sister, Patricia Hamilton-Warr, for always making me go on adventures—yesterday, today, and tomorrow.

Contents

Smuggler's Cove on the Bay of Fundy, near Yarmouth, Nova Scotia, is now a provincial park. This sheltered cove was popular with thieves and smugglers one hundred years ago.

Why are we Fascinated With Pirates?

Everyone knows pirates were thieves who would use violence to get what they wanted. Yet we enjoy watching funny pirate movies, and people of all ages love to dress up as pirates. Why are we so fascinated by them? Is it because we imagine they were rich and lived a life of fun and adventure, with lots of time at the beach? How did a typical pirate spend his or her day? Did most pirates retire somewhere warm with chests of gold and jewels? Or did they end up swinging at the end of a hangman's rope? Were pirates ruthless killers who tortured their victims for entertainment? Or were they charming and likeable characters who could talk their way out of any situation? Read on to find out the answers to these questions, and learn the real story of the pirates who sailed the seas of Atlantic Canada and beyond.

Piracy, or robbery at sea, has been around for thousands of years, since people first started travelling the oceans to move things like grain, wine, olive oil, silver, and amber from place to place by boat. In those days, if someone had something of value in their ship, there was probably someone sailing along behind them, thinking of ways to steal it.

Pirates sailed the Mediterranean Sea, along the coasts of Africa and India, around China, and up and down the entire continent of South America. The pirates based in the Caribbean Sea sailed back and forth across the Atlantic Ocean, attacking ships from European countries.

"...the age of gunpowder was not a comfortable age in which to live in coastal Nova Scotia, New Brunswick, Prince Edward Island, Quebec, or Newfoundland, with shiploads of drunken thugs out to rob you and burn your house..."

—PLUNDER AND PILLAGE: ATLANTIC CANADA'S BRUTAL & BLOODTHIRSTY PIRATES & PRIVATEERS BY HAROLD HORWOOD

Different names for "pirates" include: buccaneer, corsair, filibuster, freebooter, gentlemen of fortune, rover, and swashbuckler. Can you think of any others?

There be Pirates!

WHY WOULD SOMEONE BECOME A PIRATE?

People probably became pirates for the same reasons people today turn to a life of crime. When someone has few opportunities, crime may look like the only path to a better life. From the mid-1600s to the early 1700s (later, known as the Golden Age of Piracy), if you wanted a life at sea, there were few choices: join the **navy**, work on a **merchant ship**, become a fisherman, an explorer, or a pirate.

The pay and working conditions in the navy were terrible. Samuel Johnson, a famous eighteenth-century writer, said that being a sailor in the navy was a lot like being in jail. The work was hard, the food was bad, and life on a ship was both dull and, at times, very dangerous. But, unlike a prisoner, a sailor had a good chance of drowning! A sailor on a pirate ship had a slightly easier job than sailors in the navy, because there were more crew on a pirate ship to share the work. Sailors might become pirates when there was a chance for a quick profit, but later return to honest work. People were tempted to become pirates to get rich.

PIRATE PAY

Pirates shared their **booty** with their crew so even a cabin boy or cook could get rich from the loot stolen from a single ship. A pirate captain would receive about twice as much as a regular crew member.

This was not the case for sailors in the British navy. A captain in the navy would receive one hundred and fifty times more in salary than a common sailor. Back on dry land, a typical clerk might earn five **pounds** in a year, and an executive might earn thirty pounds in a year. A pirate could earn a thousand pounds as his share from the capture of a single ship.

By raiding just one ship loaded with valuable cargo in one day, a pirate could make as much money as most people earned in England in a year. It isn't so hard to understand why some sailors wanted to become pirates—a pirate's pay for me!

THE TYPICAL PIRATE

Most pirates were strong and healthy young men who could endure the hard, physical work that went with being a sailor. It took muscle to haul ropes, and bravery to climb up the rigging to fix sails in heavy wind or driving rain as the ship was crashing through huge waves. A sailor also had to be able to endure being cold and wet for days at a time, and living in very cramped quarters. Many ordinary pirate sailors had little formal education and could not read or write, but pirate captains were often well educated, knew how to navigate a ship, and were fearless fighters. The average age for a pirate was twenty-seven years old. The average age for a pirate captain was forty years old. Pirates tended to die young from drowning, injury, or infection. Only a few lucky or smart pirates got to retire with their booty.

Alwilda, the First Female Pirate (5th century)

Was Alwilda a real person or is she just a story? To avoid having to marry the man her father had picked for her, Alwilda and some of her friends escaped on a ship. At sea, this all-female crew took over another ship full of pirates and Alwilda became their captain.

Alwilda and her crew were such successful pirates that Prince Alf of Denmark was given the job of putting a stop to them. And he did. Prince Alf caught and captured them, killed most of the crew, and took Alwilda prisoner. Alwilda was so impressed with his bravery that she decided to marry him.

Funny thing is, Prince Alf was the man that Alwilda's father wanted her to marry in the first place. As the story goes, they married and Alwilda became the queen of Denmark.

A DAY IN THE LIFE OF A PIRATE

Life on a pirate ship was usually pretty boring, unless there was another ship on the horizon. Pirates would often follow a ship for hours trying to decide if it was worth capturing. Is it full of treasure, or might it have needed supplies? Does it have lots of cannons, guns, and sailors? Can it be caught? While the captain and **quartermaster** studied the other ship with a **telescope**, the crew prepared to fight. Once a battle begins, there is no pause in the action.

A pirate ship has way more crew than a **vessel** that carries cargo. With fewer men to defeat, the battle is likely to be quick and violent. But if the other captain surrenders, there will be no need to fight. The next few days will be spent moving everything of value on to the pirate ship. Once the booty has been moved, the quartermaster will divvy everything up and each man will get his share, according to the **articles**.

The average day for a pirate all depended on what was on the horizon.

If there was no ship in sight, it might be just another quiet day. Playing dice or cards helped pass the time. Some sailors were good storytellers, others could entertain the crew with a song or a dance. If the sea was calm, there may be time for a nap. If you were lucky, there would be something to eat. Food on a pirate ship was usually scarce and often so bad that the sailors would prefer to eat in the dark so they couldn't see the insects squirming around in their food. Alcohol was plentiful and helped to keep their spirits high and to give the pirates enough energy to survive times of little food.

The life of a pirate could be full of adventure, or really dull. It just depended on what was on the horizon.

Who Would Have Guessed that Pirates liked to Read Adventure Stories?

In 2018, books were found on Blackbeard's ship, *Queen Anne's Revenge*. The pirate's ship hit a sandbar and sank in 1718. Since the wreck was discovered in 1996, thousands of interesting things have been recovered and brought up from the bottom of the ocean including a brass bell, a gun, a sword, cannon balls, and cannons. Scientists were curious about sixteen pieces of paper, each smaller than a loonie, found inside one of the cannons. On seven of the pieces, they could read the words and proved that they were from a book. The book, published in 1712, was *A Voyage to the South Sea, and Round the World, Perform'd in the Years 1708, 1709, 1710 and 1711* by Captain Edward Cooke.

On your next trip, be like a pirate and pack a good adventure story.

CHAPTER 1

The History of Piracy

I n Ancient Greece, more than two thousand years ago, stealing from other ships was simply a way to get rich. For instance, in the story *The Odyssey* by the Greek poet Homer, the hero, Odysseus, brags about how many ships he has raided. Odysseus probably didn't think of himself as a pirate, but his victims were robbed at sea, which is the definition of piracy.

HOW DO WE KNOW SO MUCH ABOUT PIRATES?

Today, we know a great deal about pirates because there have been decades to gather stories, and there were even several books about pirates written during the Golden Age of Piracy. One of the first books, *The Buccaneers of America* by Alexandre Exquemelin, was published in 1678. His book was first published in Dutch, translated into German and Spanish, and then English in 1684. The author had insider information based on twelve years of being a doctor and sailing with pirates, including the infamous Captain Henry Morgan. Exquemelin was a part of Morgan's most famous attack on Porto Bello, in what is now Panama. Today, we are not sure if the book is totally accurate because some of the original information from the first edition was mistranslated and changed by the time it was published in English.

In 1724, *A General History of the Robberies and Murders of the Most Notorious Pyrates* was published. This book, sometimes referred to as *A General History of the Pyrates*, included information about lots of famous pirates like Blackbeard, William Kidd, Mary Read, Bartholomew Roberts, and Anne Bonny. The book included details about punishments, tortures, hangings, clothing, and food aboard pirate ships and is the reason so much is known about many of the pirates examined in this book. There is some controversy over who is the actual author of this book, but most historians agree that it was written by Captain Charles Johnson.

Stories about pirates often painted a very different picture of what life was actually like for them. From reading these stories, you would think life was easy and that a chest of pirate treasure was buried on every island in the Caribbean. The writers of the opera *The*

There be Pirates!

Pirates of Penzance, which was first performed in 1879, created such an entertaining view of pirate life that it had everyone singing "it is a glorious thing to be a pirate king." Facts about pirates have been mixed in with stories so much that sometimes it is difficult to know what is true and what is fantasy.

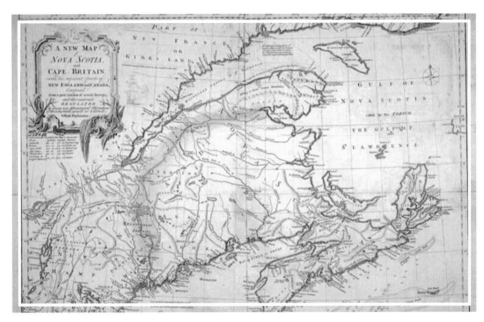

Map of Nova Scotia, Prince Edward Island, and New Brunswick, created in 1755 by Thomas Jeffreys, shortly after the Golden Age of Piracy.

PIRACY IN THE NORTH ATLANTIC

Some sailors we now call "pirates" likely never thought of themselves that way. The captains of private ships could receive a license, or letter of marque, from their government that encouraged them to attack and raid enemy ships. By doing this, a king would have all of the benefits of a navy, with none of the costs. These sailors were called **privateers** and were supposed to give the treasure from captured ships to their government. A pirate got to keep all of the booty when they plundered a ship. There were many famous sea captains who started out as privateers but became pirates.

The earliest European explorers claimed places they "discovered"—even if there were already people living there—on behalf of their king and country. The New World (the name for North America, the islands of the Caribbean, and Central and South America) was considered a prize to be taken by the strongest European nation. Some writers have called the earliest explorers pirates for taking what they wanted without any regard for the people already there.

Newfoundland and the rest of coastal Atlantic Canada was fought over by explorers, privateers, and pirates from many European countries who wanted to control the land and the fisheries. The story of pirates in Atlantic Canada begins in Newfoundland.

PETER EASTON, THE PIRATE ADMIRAL (1570–1620)

Peter Easton was one of the most successful and powerful pirates of all time and made his home base in Newfoundland in the early 1600s. Easton began his sailing career as a privateer, then turned pirate. He had a fleet of dozens of ships and had hundreds of men under his command. Unlike most pirates of the time, Easton had a reputation for NOT killing the people he stole from. While many tried, no one was able to capture him.

PETER EASTON

PETER EASTON "THE PIRATE ADMIRAL" FORTIFIED THIS SITE IN 1610 AND MADE NEWFOUNDLAND HIS BASE UNTIL 1614. HE DEFEATED A FRENCH SQUADRON AT HARBOUR GRACE IN 1611, RECRUITED 5,000 FISHERMEN FROM THIS COLONY INTO HIS CREWS, AND RAIDED FOREIGN SHIPPING AS FAR AS THE CARIBBEAN. IN 1614 HE INTERCEPTED THE SPANISH PLATE FLEET AT THE AZORES, CAPTURED THREE TREASURE SHIPS, AND DIVIDED AN IMMENSE FORTUNE AMONG HIS CREWS. HE WAS TWICE PARDONED AND INVITED HOME BY JAMES I, BUT RETIRED INSTEAD TO SOUTHERN FRANCE WHERE HE BECAME MARQUIS OF SAVOY AND LIVED IN GREAT SPLENDOR.

ERECTED BY THEIR FRIENDS IN MEMORY OF JEROME C. & PAMELA E. BARTON LEE FIRST CURATOR CONCEPTION BAY MUSEUM 1974

A plaque from the Conception Bay Museum in Harbour Grace, Newfoundland, said to be the only plaque in Canada honouring a pirate.

Easton first visited Newfoundland in 1602 as part of a **convoy** that protected the fishing fleet. Because he was working for the queen of England, he could simply ask the locals for additional men and supplies and it was the duty of loyal subjects to oblige. If people didn't volunteer supplies, Easton was legally entitled to take what he needed and force men to join his crew.

But when England and Spain declared peace in 1604, Peter Easton became a pirate. He attacked any ship, including those from his own country, in the waters around England. When King James I appointed Henry Mainwaring, an English sailor, to put a stop to him, Easton sailed for Africa where pirates had few enemies and there were lots of easy targets to steal from. From Africa, he sailed all the way to Newfoundland and made his base first in Harbour Grace, then in Ferryland. He captured and plundered the fleet that was carrying gold and silver back to Spain from the New World.

The First Pirate Flag

What we now think of as the typical "pirate flag" (black background with a white skull and crossbones) first appeared more than 2,000 years ago. Cilician pirates from the Mediterranean used the skull and crossbones to frighten and intimidate their victims into surrendering. (See page 24 for more about pirate flags.)

There be Pirates!

SAYING NO TO A PIRATE

For eleven weeks, Peter Easton tried to convince Richard Whitbourne, an English government official, to provide him with men and supplies, promising to make Whitbourne rich if he helped. Easton held Whitbourne captive on his ship and tried to bribe him with good food and wine, but Whitbourne politely refused all of Easton's requests. He knew if he agreed to help Easton, it would make him a pirate too.

Easton finally let Whitbourne go after he agreed to help Easton get a **pardon**. Anyone accused of being a pirate would be persecuted and treated like a criminal, but the king could give anyone a pardon so he or she would not be punished. King James I agreed to issue a pardon, but we are not sure if Easton ever officially received it. In 1620, Richard Whitbourne published a book about his time in Newfoundland and being held hostage by Peter Easton.

Peter Easton eventually retired to the south of France with his treasure. Many people think that some of the vast treasure of Peter Easton, the Pirate Admiral, may still be buried in several different locations in Newfoundland.

Sheila NaGeira, Newfoundland's Princess

On his way to Newfoundland, Captain Peter Easton and his crew captured a Dutch ship only to find that it was already holding captives. Easton rescued the prisoners and took them with him to Newfoundland. One of the passengers, Sheila O'Connor, was actually an Irish princess. Her father was heir to the throne of Connaught, and she was known as Sheila NaGeira, which is Gaelic for "Sheila the Beautiful".

On the long voyage, Sheila fell in love with and married Gilbert Pike, one of Easton's officers. Gilbert decided to quit being a pirate and he and Sheila stayed in Newfoundland, living in Harbour Grace before settling in Carbonear.

Many believe that the stories of Sheila NaGeira are just legends told by generations of Newfoundlanders. But Pike is a very common name in Newfoundland and many people claim to trace their roots to Princess Sheila and Gilbert Pike.

HENRY MAINWARING: OXFORD SCHOLAR TURNED PIRATE (1587–1653)

Henry Mainwaring was from an important English family and graduated from Oxford University before becoming a sailor. King James I of England gave him the job of trying to stop Peter Easton. When he learned that Easton had stopped raiding ships off the coast of England, Mainwaring changed the target and headed south to raid Spanish ships off the coast of Africa. The man who set out to capture the pirate Peter Easton was now a pirate himself.

There be Pirates!

When he was ready to give up being a pirate, Mainwaring made a deal with King James I. He paid a huge sum of money to the king and received a pardon for being a pirate. The king knighted him and made him an officer in the Royal Navy. Mainwaring's new job was to put a stop to piracy and, as you might have guessed, he was good at that, thanks to his first-hand experience as a pirate! He convinced the king to stop offering pardons to pirates and instead offer rewards to people who could capture pirate ships. The former pirate, now called Sir Henry Mainwaring, wrote a book about how to stop piracy and a manual for sailors called *The Seaman's Dictionary.*

GRACE O'MALLEY, PIRATE QUEEN OF IRELAND (1530–1603)

Grace O'Malley was born in Ireland around 1530. Her nickname in Irish **Gaelic** was "Graneaille" (pronounced Gran-u-ale), which meant "bald," because she kept her hair cut short, an uncommon thing for a young woman. Unlike most females of the time, Grace received a solid education and could speak Latin, the language spoken by educated people across Europe. Grace eventually married, had children, and took over command of her father's ships when he died. She continued his work to keep Ireland safe from the English, who were trying to take Irish land and force its people to swear allegiance to the queen of England. Grace fought to keep the English out of Ireland, but in 1577 she was captured and kept in an English jail for over a year. Once released, she returned to defending Ireland from the English. After many years of fighting, and seeing her own sons captured, Grace knew she had to surrender, but was determined to do it her own way. Grace sailed across the Irish Sea to England and right up the River Thames to London so that she could speak directly with Queen Elizabeth I. The queen was impressed and in 1593 awarded Grace and her people a royal pardon. Grace, the Pirate Queen of Ireland, died in 1603.

Why couldn't the pirate play cards?
Because he was standing on the deck.

CHAPTER 2
Pirate life

Most crew members on a pirate ship were sailors who left the harsh conditions common on navy ships, or the difficult life on a fishing boat or a merchant vessel.

But not all aboard a pirate ship were there voluntarily. Some were forced to become pirates when their ship was captured. The other options were to stay on a floundering ship that had been stripped of all its supplies, or face death at the end of a **cutlass**. Captives with special skills, such as a carpenter or a barber surgeon (see page 49), were often forced onto a pirate ship and made to work at their trade. Once a sailor signed the articles (see page 28), rules that all sailors followed, they were considered by the rest of the crew to be one of them.

Some refused to sign the articles because this would mean that they would be punished with the rest of the crew if they were captured and brought to trial. The punishment for the crime of piracy was to be hanged. In some places, the pirate's dead body was also placed in a cage called a gibbet (see page 50) at the harbour entrance as a warning to other would-be pirates.

NO PREY, NO PAY

For a pirate, the rule was "no prey, no pay." In order to make money, pirates had to hunt, attack, and steal from other ships. No one was paying them to deliver a cargo, carry passengers, or defend their country.

Like in the navy, it took a great deal of skill and work to maintain and navigate a pirate ship. The sail master, or navigator, read the charts, and used the **compass**, telescope, **astrolabe**, cross staff, and other instruments to navigate the ship and direct the sailors. The people who could navigate the ship were called "sea artists."

A compass, telescope, ship's log, and sea chart were important for navigating a pirate ship.

There be Pirates!

For a pirate, the rule was, "no prey, no pay."

The **boatswain**, or bosun, was in charge of keeping everything ship shape, especially all of the ropes that were an essential part of sailing. The gunner trained the crew to operate the cannons and made sure that there was always a supply of ammunition. Anyone with the special skills required for these jobs was in demand and could easily find work on a ship. If the pirates needed someone with these skills, they would force them to join their crew.

Decision-making on a pirate ship was a democratic process. Every crew member had a vote on where they went and who they would attack. It was only during a battle or when the ship was chasing another ship—or being chased—that the captain had full authority. The

Painting of William Kidd by Howard Pyle.

There be Pirates!

quartermaster was also elected by the crew and was the second-in-command on the ship. The quartermaster had many important duties. He would lead the attacks, divide up the loot, settle arguments, and decide on the punishments. It was the quartermaster who ensured that everything aboard ship was done fairly and he made sure that the captain was aware of any rumblings from the crew. If the crew were dissatisfied with the captain or quartermaster, they could vote to replace them.

The crew, as a group, decided on the day-to-day rules, or articles, that everyone had to follow. These articles helped to keep everyone on board safe and to prevent fights. They covered everything from where smoking was allowed to how to divide the loot. Many of the pirate articles are similar because pirate ships often travelled

What is the Pirate Round?

In the Golden Age of Piracy, ships would sail from the coast of North America across the Atlantic Ocean, down the coast of Africa, around the Cape of Good Hope at the tip of the African continent, and up into the Indian Ocean. Once there, pirates stole what they could from ships filled with goods from India, Ethiopia, Egypt, and the East Indies, before heading back to sell their exotic loot in Boston or New York. This loop around the bottom of the continent of Africa and back to North America was called the Pirate Round. A skilled pirate captain and a brave crew could get very rich if they could successfully make the Pirate Round.

Pirate Life

Pirate Flags

When you think of a pirate flag, a skull and crossbones is what usually comes to mind. These are symbols of death and can still be seen on very old headstones. The first flags used by pirates were probably solid black, which meant that you should surrender without fighting. A solid red flag signified that they would show no mercy, or that all of their victims were going to die. The term "Jolly Roger" is thought to have come from the French *jolie rouge* or "pretty red" or "Old Roger," a term for the devil. If a flag had an hourglass, it meant that your time was running out.

in groups and the captains would meet to exchange information and ideas (see page 28).

BARTHOLOMEW ROBERTS, THE MOST SUCCESSFUL PIRATE (1682–1722)

"In honest service there is thin rations, low wages and hard labour; in this, plenty and satiety, pleasure and ease, liberty and power…No, a merry life and a short one shall be my motto."

—BARTHOLOMEW ROBERTS, *A GENERAL HISTORY OF THE ROBBERIES AND MURDERS OF THE MOST NOTORIOUS PYRATES* WRITTEN BY CAPTAIN CHARLES JOHNSON IN 1724

Bartholomew Roberts lived up to his motto of living a short life. He became a pirate when he was in his late thirties, declaring that if he was going to be a pirate, he may as well be captain. After his death, he was given the name "Black Bart" and has become known as the sea's most successful pirate ever. He captured more ships than anyone else, even though his career as a pirate lasted only three years.

Roberts was born in Wales in 1682, but little is known about his life before 1719, when the ship he was working on was captured by pirate Howell Davis. When Davis was killed in a raid, Roberts was elected by the crew to become captain. As captain, Roberts was daring and bold, and an excellent navigator. His favourite tactic for capturing ships was simply to sail into the midst of a convoy and invite the captain of one of the ships aboard for a meeting. Over drinks, he would ask the captain which ship in the convoy had the most valuable cargo. If the captain co-operated, he would be set free and Roberts and his crew would steal everything of value—like gold, sugar, and tobacco—from the other ship.

In the summer of 1720, Roberts plundered more than

Modern interpretation of Bartholomew Roberts.

twenty ships in Trepassey Bay, south of what is now St. John's, Newfoundland. Roberts and his crew sailed into the bay while the musicians on their ship played at full volume. The sailors on the other ships must have thought that the crew on this unknown ship were just happy to be in port and paid them no attention. Once in the harbour, Roberts and his crew started firing their cannons at the ships already at anchor, and attacked other ships entering the bay. When the shooting was over, the pirates had sunk or captured twenty-six ships. For two weeks, Roberts and his crew controlled the small port. We do know that several local men joined him when he and his crew sailed out of Trepassey Bay in one of the best ships in the harbour.

No one knows exactly what Bartholomew Roberts looked like but Captain Charles Johnson tells us in his book that Roberts liked to wear fancy clothes (see page 27), that he preferred to drink tea rather than rum, and the time for lights out was specified in his articles.

In 1722, Roberts was killed at the beginning of a bloody battle with the crew of a navy ship. Without the leadership of their captain, the pirates knew they couldn't win and gave up. Before they were captured, Roberts's crew followed his wishes and threw their black flag and

There be Pirates!

Roberts's body overboard. No sailor, not even a pirate, wanted to have their flag captured by the enemy after losing a battle. If Roberts's body had been found on the ship after the battle, it would have been taken by the navy sailors. When they returned to port, it would have been put in a gibbet (see page 50) as a warning to other pirates. No pirate wanted to end up in a gibbet, it was far better to be buried at sea. While we know that Black Bart's life was short, we are left to wonder just how merry it was.

> *"Roberts himself made a gallant figure at the time of the engagement, being dressed in a rich crimson damask waistcoat and breeches, a red feather in his hat, a gold chain around his neck, with a diamond cross hanging to it, a sword in his hand and two pair of pistols, hanging at the end of a silk sling, flung over his shoulders"*
>
> —A General History of the Robberies and Murders of the most notorious Pyrates by Captain Charles Johnson

FOOD ON A PIRATE SHIP

Before setting out on a long sea voyage, sailors would load their ship with just enough **provisions** to last until

The Pirate Articles of Bartholomew Roberts

In today's language, here are Black Bart's articles:

1. Every man on the ship has a vote on the decisions to be made and all food and drink will be shared equally among everyone on board.
2. The plunder will be divided fairly. The punishment for taking more than your share will be marooning. Anyone who steals from another sailor will have their nose and ears sliced and may also be **marooned**.
3. Playing cards or dice for money is forbidden.
4. Lights out at eight o'clock. After lights out, alcohol is to be consumed on deck and in the dark.
5. Every man must keep all of his weapons clean and ready for battle.
6. No children or women are allowed on the ship.
7. Anyone who tries to leave the ship during a battle will be killed or marooned.
8. No fighting between members of the crew is permitted on the ship. You can have a duel on shore, if necessary.
9. No one can quit, or even talk about quitting, until each person on board has received their share of 1,000 pounds. Anyone injured in the line of duty will receive extra shares. (See pirate insurance, page 49.)
10. All plunder will be shared as follows: the captain and the quartermaster will each receive two shares, the master gunner and the boatswain will receive one and a half shares, other officers will receive one and a quarter shares, the rest of the crew shall receive one share each.
11. The musicians have Sunday off but will play as and when requested, the other six days of the week.

Historians say that many pirates had similar articles and flags because pirate captains would meet and share news and ideas. Edward Low had a special flag, called the green trumpeter, that he would raise as a signal for other captains to come to his ship.

What is Davy Jones's Locker?

Davy Jones's Locker is a place—the bottom of the ocean. Sailors use the term when talking about someone drowning or a ship sinking and ending up in "Davy Jones's Locker." This is not a place where any pirate wants to end up!

they reached their destination. Space in the cargo hold of a ship was limited, so there was always a chance they would run out of food far from land. Sometimes food and drink were rationed and everyone had to do with eating less.

Even though they were surrounded by the ocean, drinking water was always in short supply. After sitting in barrels for a long time, the water tasted terrible. Beer and rum lasted longer because of the alcohol, and were the preferred drinks of sailors.

Since there was no refrigeration, fish and meat were salted and kept in big barrels. Live animals, such as pigs, goats, and chickens, were loaded on board. Chicken eggs, sometimes called "cackle fruit," were a popular food for pirates.

When the food supply was really low, sailors would catch and eat rats. Interestingly, some sailors reported that rats didn't taste too bad.

Cooking on a pirate ship was not easy. Imagine trying to make all of your meals over an open fire, like when you're camping, but having to do it inside a very small, dark, cramped space the size of a closet. Preparing everything in a single pot was easiest for the cook, so pirates ate a lot of stew and porridge. Imagine the work involved in keeping a fire going. There was no "on" button to start a stove in the galley of a pirate ship.

On the morning of his last battle, we know that Bartholomew Roberts ate a stew called **salmagundi**. No doubt he dipped a piece of hardtack into his stew. Hardtack is a thick cracker baked until it is very dry and rock hard so that it can last a very long time and has been a staple on ships for hundreds of years. People

Clothes Make the Pirate?

We know that Captain Bartholomew Roberts dressed in beautiful clothes before a battle and looked like a fine gentleman. Everyday sailors wore loose fitting, comfortable clothing made of rough sailcloth so that they could climb the rigging to adjust the sails or swab the deck. As a form of protection from the weather and during a sword fight, they would wear coats covered in **pitch** that made them thick and stiff. A pirate would wear the same pants and shirt, day after day. After a successful battle, pirates would steal the best clothes from their victims. As was the style during the Golden Age of Piracy, gentlemen of the time wore linen or silk shirts trimmed with lace, satin **breeches**, and coats of fine wool or velvet.

still eat hardtack and you can buy it in some stores in Atlantic Canada today.

Eat like a Pirate—Make Your Own Hardtack

Warning: This is a tricky recipe! If you aren't ready to clean up a mess, don't try this! Instead, check to see if your grocery store sells hardtack.

Ingredients

2 to 2 ½ cups (500–625mls) of flour
1 cup (250mls) of warm water
1 teaspoon (5mls) of salt

Directions

Preheat oven to 350°F.

Put 2 cups (500mls) of the flour and the salt into a large bowl and stir. Add the water. Mix with a spoon until the dough starts to come together into the shape of a ball, adding more flour if it is too sticky.

Once the dough stops sticking to the sides of the bowl, sprinkle some flour onto a piece of wax paper on your counter, then put the ball of dough on the floured wax paper. Sprinkle a bit more flour on top and knead, or mix together, with your hands.
Keep kneading and adding flour until the dough is not sticky and feels smooth.

Use a rolling pin to roll the dough into the shape of a small pizza about a half centimetre thick. When the dough stops sticking and you can move it around on the wax paper, use a toothpick to poke holes in the dough, then cut the dough into cracker-sized pieces.

Place the individual pieces on a cookie sheet, making sure that they are not too close together. You may need to use a second cookie sheet. Bake for about 25 minutes, then take out of the oven to test. They should be firm, and the tops should be a very light brown colour. You may need to bake for another 5 minutes.

Use a spatula to remove half of the squares and let them cool on a wire rack. This batch of hardtack will be more like crackers and you can eat them on their own or covered in something tasty like peanut butter.
Put the cookie sheet back in the oven with the last half of the crackers and cook for 20 more minutes. You may need to bake for an additional 5 minutes so that they are nice and brown on top and cooked inside.

There be Pirates!

Take out and cool for at least 30 minutes. This hardtack will be really hard when cooled. If you store it in an air-tight container in a cool place it will keep for a long time.

Eat like a pirate by dunking some hardtack into salmagundi, soup, or a glass of milk.

~~~~~~

Woodes Rogers, Pirate Catcher (1679–1732)

Captain Woodes Rogers was an author, a privateer, and—some say—a pirate. Rogers's father spent time in Newfoundland in the early 1700s and some historians say that Woodes was there with his father on some of his voyages. He is credited with being an excellent captain who survived mutinies and shipwrecks, captured twenty ships, and kept fighting in battles even after being shot in the face.

Woodes is best known as the person who drove pirates out of the Bahamas, after being appointed governor of the island in 1717. The entire island of New Providence, and especially the port of Nassau, was a well-known pirate lair and Rogers guessed that many of the men there would agree to abandon piracy if he offered them land and would not punish them for their crimes. Most of the pirates there took the pardon and land but some pirates, such as Blackbeard, simply sailed away and never returned. Any pirates that remained fought hard to keep Rogers out of Nassau. Rogers defeated the remaining pirates and hanged eight of them. With great effort, he rebuilt the town and the fort. Captain Woodes Rogers is credited with bringing on the end of the Golden Age of Piracy by driving the pirates out of the Bahamas.

There be Pirates!

CHAPTER 3

Destruction, Dismemberment, and Death

"Dead cats don't mew. You know what to do."

—Pirate Captain Pedro Gilbert, *The Pirates* by Douglas Botting

Pirates were unpredictable and most were incredibly violent. If you had something a pirate wanted, you had a few choices: you could give it up without a fight and you might live another day, or you could surrender the valuables and the pirates might kill you anyway. The saying "dead men tell no tales" is a practice that many pirates followed.

EDWARD LOW, THE CRUELLEST PIRATE (APPROXIMATELY 1690–1724)

Edward Low is known as the cruellest and most brutal of all the pirates in the Golden Age of Piracy. He was born in Westminster, England, sometime around 1690. Low worked at a shipyard but was eventually fired and returned to his old job as a sailor. He soon tired of working hard, being hungry, and making little money, so he convinced a few fellow sailors they should steal a small boat and become pirates.

Skull and crossbones on a headstone at the Old Burial Ground in Chester, Nova Scotia.

One of Low's first raids took place near Shelburne, Nova Scotia, in 1722 or 1723. Low and his crew sailed right into Port Roseway (Shelburne's name at the time) between thirteen unsuspecting New England fishing ships. The forty-four pirates, led by Low, threatened to kill

There be Pirates!

anyone who didn't immediately surrender. More than a hundred scared fishermen gave up without a fight. Low took the largest of the fishing **schooners** as his own, added guns to it, and changed its name from the *Mary* to the *Fancy*. After three days of looting he and his crew sailed away from Shelburne, bound for Newfoundland.

Now with a ship fit for a pirate, Captain Edward Low sailed up and down the eastern seaboard of North America, back and forth across the Atlantic, and around the Caribbean. One of his favourite tricks was to fly a false flag to get close to ships that might be carrying valuable cargo. During his few years as a pirate, Low captured and plundered more than a hundred ships, almost half of them in the waters of what is now Atlantic Canada.

The Man who Silenced Edward Low

During a particularly vicious attack on a captured ship, Edward Low was accidentally injured by one of his own men. His cheek was sliced so wide open that you could actually see his teeth, even when his mouth was closed! The barber surgeon on board stitched up the cut but didn't do a great job. Low went berserk hurling insults and abuse at him. The barber surgeon responded like a true pirate and punched Low in the face, tearing out the new stitches. Since the barber surgeon was irreplaceable, he wasn't punished, and Low had to keep quiet. Edward Low, one of the cruellest pirates ever, was left with an ugly scar and, perhaps, a newfound respect for the barber surgeon.

Destruction, Dismemberment, and Death

Low was reputed to have killed fifty-three people in one brutal attack. He earned his reputation as the cruellest pirate of his time by torturing his victims for entertainment. The forms of torture included hanging people from the mast of the ship by their wrists, cutting the nose and lips off one unfortunate rival, and slicing the ears off another.

Low's career as a pirate was very violent, but short, and nothing more is known about him after 1724. Historians differ on how he died. Some say his crew was so disgusted with his increasing violence that they finally **mutinied** and put Low in a small boat without any food or water and left him to die. Others say that he was rescued and, when the sailors learned who he was, he was turned over to the authorities, tried for piracy, and hanged. In another version, his

Revenge Privateer

Commanded by Capt. *James Gandy* Who has been on several Cruizes and met a great Success.

All Gentlemen Volunteers ; Seamen, and able bodied Landfmen, who wish to acquire Riches and Honor, are invited to repair on board the *Revenge Privateer* fhip of War, now laying in *Halifax* Harbour ; mounting Thirty Carriage Guns, with Cahorns, swivels, &c. bound on a Cruize to the Southward for four Months against the French and all His Majesty's Enemies, and then to return to this Harbour.

All Volunteers will be received on board the faid fhip -- or by Captain *James Gandy* at his Rendezvous at *Mr. Proud's* Tavern near the Market Houfe, where they will meet with all due Encouragement, and the best Treatment ; Proper Advance will be given.

GOD fave the KING.

A replica of a newspaper ad used to recruit pirates, from the January 12, 1779, edition of the *Nova Scotia Gazette*.

There be Pirates!

ship sank in a storm and all aboard died. Some say that Edward Low was never caught.

Marooning

A pirate accused of stealing from another pirate could face one of the worst of all punishments, marooning. He would be left on a tiny bit of land in the middle of the ocean with nothing more than a small bottle of water, a gun, but very little ammunition, and no way to build a fire. The certain fate for most marooned pirates was a slow death by dehydration and starvation. Fictional accounts of marooning, however, made it sound like a lot of fun. In *Robinson Crusoe*, written by Daniel Defoe in 1719, the main character spent more than twenty-five years on an island, having various adventures, before being rescued. This book has been made into movies, plays, and graphic novels. There are hundreds of print versions of this story and it has been translated into several languages, including Inuktitut. The movie *Cast Away*, starring Tom Hanks, is a modern-day Robinson Crusoe story.

WRECKERS: PIRATES BY CHANCE

What would people on land do if they saw a ship caught up in a storm and about to crash on jagged rocks? Most did what they could to help the ship avoid danger. If a ship crashed, they would risk their own lives to rescue the sailors. But not all were so helpful. Some would light a fire to lure ships onto a rocky shore, hoping it would crash. This was called "wrecking" and the people who did it were called "wreckers." Wreckers would loot the

Destruction, Dismemberment, and Death

cargo, keep what they wanted, and sell the rest. This happened all over Atlantic Canada in the 1600 and 1700s. Sometimes people who lived on the coast would act like pirates themselves, when they had the chance.

The Graveyard of the Atlantic

Sable Island, off the coast of Nova Scotia, was known as the Graveyard of the Atlantic because so many ships sank there. To try to keep ships and their crews safe, the government established a rescue station on the island in 1801.

WRECK OF THE "ARCADIA," ON SABLE ISLAND.

A wreck off Sable Island, by artist A. Hill, as it appeared in *Ballou's Pictorial* newspaper on January 24, 1857.

There be Pirates!

Wearing a "Checkered" Shirt

A common punishment was getting whipped with something called "a cat of nine tails." Nine pieces of rope were attached to a handle, and when a sailor was whipped on the back, the skin would be cut in a checkered pattern. No sailor wanted to wear this checkered shirt.

Carry Your Booty like a Pirate— Make Your Own Pouch
Difficulty level: medium

Sailors carried their valuables in a pouch. Follow these directions and make a pouch to hold your pirate booty.

Supplies: piece of leather or felt about 17cm by 17cm, shoelace or ribbon about 1 metre long, scissors, saucer or bowl.

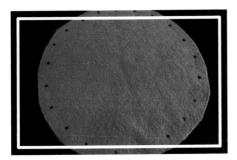

1. Find a saucer or bowl that is slightly smaller than the piece of leather or felt.
2. Trace around the bowl, then cut out the circle.
3. Mark an even number of dots around the edge of the circle, about 3cm apart and about 1cm from the edge of the circle.

4. Fold the material in half and, at each dot, use scissors to make a small cut parallel to the edge of the circle. This is the trickiest part, so ask an adult to help.
5. Thread a shoelace or piece of ribbon through each hole.

Destruction, Dismemberment, and Death

6. Pull both ends of the laces or ribbon to close the pouch and secure it with a simple knot.

7. Attach the pouch to your belt or belt loop.

Now you can store your treasure like a pirate!

Walking the Plank

If asked to name a common pirate torture, most landlubbers would say, "walk the plank." While this didn't happen on a real pirate ship, it is included in many pirate stories such as *Peter Pan* and *Treasure Island*. This myth started after the publication *The Pirates' Own Book: Authentic Narratives of the Most Celebrated Sea Robbers*, written by Charles Ellms in 1837.

There be Pirates!

CHAPTER 4
Tools of the Trade

NAVIGATION

Today, if you need to go somewhere you have never visited before, you would probably use the GPS (global positioning system) built into your cellphone. An app will show you a route on a map. Imagine how difficult it would be to follow a map when in the middle of the ocean. There are no road signs or landmarks telling a sailor to go two thousand kilometres, then turn left to get to Oak Island, or even the great harbours at Boston or New York. So how did pirates navigate across oceans, into bays, and up rivers?

An octant from the late 1700s.

Hundreds of years ago, sailors relied on common sense, good luck, and some basic tools to find their way. Pirates used a compass and a chart, or map, showing the sea coast and known islands. But a sea chart was of little use to anyone who couldn't read, a common thing for most pirates. By using an astrolabe, back staff, or cross staff, then later an octant, quadrant, or sextant, a skilled sailor could tell where he was from the location of the sun and the stars.

A lookout standing at the top of a mast could see for about fifteen to thirty kilometres. Invented near the

Sea Charts

Sea charts and tools were of such value that they were one of the first things that pirates stole when they captured a ship. When pirate Bartholomew Sharp (1650–1690) captured a Spanish ship full of silver, the most valuable thing on board was a set of sea charts. To keep the charts out of enemy hands, the Spanish sailors tried to throw the charts overboard. Sharp stole the charts and later traded them to gain his freedom when he was charged with being a pirate.

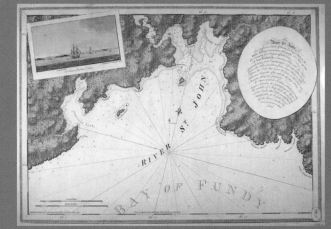

River St. John by J.F.W. DesBarres, 1780, showing where the St. John River enters the Bay of Fundy, at the present city of Saint John, New Brunswick.

There be Pirates!

end of the 1500s, a telescope was used to observe birds, which helped determine a ship's distance from land. Studying the shape and movement of clouds could help to tell the direction of the wind and the coming weather. Amazingly, using the most basic of tools, skilled pirates could sail to the exact place they wanted to go.

SHIP SHAPE SHIPS

Pirate ships had to be in good shape in order to catch other ships full of treasure and valuable goods that could be used or sold for a quick profit. While pirate ships were often smaller than the ships they hunted, their crews had three to four times more people and lots of weapons. Often the sailors on a captured ship would give up without a fight because they were so badly outnumbered and outgunned by the pirates.

In between capturing other ships and stealing their

Low and high tide in St. Martins, New Brunswick, showing why the Bay of Fundy was the perfect place for careening ships (see page 47).

treasure, sailors on pirate ships were kept busy with repairing sails and ropes, cleaning guns, and sharpening swords. Because there were so many more sailors on a pirate ship, there was less work for each sailor to do. Life on board a pirate ship was easier, but this led to boredom. Sailors with too much time on their hands often fought with each other.

Careening Ships in the Bay of Fundy

Port Royal, Jamaica, and Nassau, in the Bahamas, were busy pirate **havens**, but pirates of the North Atlantic favoured the Bay of Fundy. To keep their ships seaworthy, sailors needed to repair their ships by patching leaks and scraping the **barnacles** off the bottom of their boats. How can you fix the bottom of a boat when it is floating in water?

Today, a big ship can go into a **dry dock**, or a crane can lift a sailboat right out of the water. Hundreds of years ago, the crew of a ship would sail into a bay at high tide and wait. Once the tide went out, the ship would sit on its side, on the now exposed sea bottom. This was called **careening**. With the highest tides in the world at twelve to fifteen metres, the Bay of Fundy was the perfect place to career a ship. Pirate Edward Low used the Minas Basin to career his ships.

WILLIAM DAMPIER (APPROX. 1651–1715)

William Dampier sailed all the way around the world three times before he died in 1715. One of his first voyages was from England to Newfoundland, but he found the weather in the North Atlantic too cold for his liking. He sailed with pirates for many years, mainly in the warmer waters of the Far East, but preferred to think of himself as a privateer. He was known for the cruel way that he treated the men on his ship, and for destroying the villages and killing the people he encountered as he raided the North Atlantic coast. His success as an

Tools of the Trade

explorer and author got him the job as leader of an expedition, but it ended with his ship sinking and Dampier being **court-martialled**. While sailing around the world, Dampier made detailed drawings

A telescope was nicknamed a "bring 'em near."

and notes, which he used to write several books describing his voyages. History showed that he was a terrible captain but a brilliant navigator, explorer, and writer.

MEDICINE ON BOARD

Living conditions on ships were so terrible that more sailors died from disease, **malnutrition**, and infection than were killed while attacking another ship. Next to sea charts and navigational equipment, medicine was one of the things that pirates loved to find on a captured ship. Blackbeard is reported to have traded several ships that he and others had captured when they blockaded the Charleston Harbour, in exchange for a chest of medicine.

There be Pirates!

Some historians say that the current value of such a chest of medicine would be almost half a million dollars.

One of the most important people on the ship was the barber surgeon. It would be unusual to have a

Pirate Insurance

Sailors injured on the job were paid according to the severity of their injury:

Loss of an eye or finger	100 gold coins
Loss of a leg	400 gold coins
Loss of left arm	500 gold coins
Loss of right arm	600 gold coins

university-trained doctor, or physician, on board, so the ship's barber surgeon would "fix" a badly injured arm or leg by cutting it off with the same tools he used to pull teeth or cut hair. While this might have saved the injured sailor's life in the short term, most pirates who were badly hurt eventually died from infection.

MARGARET JORDAN, BRUTAL PIRATE OR UNWILLING ACCOMPLICE?

In the summer of 1809, the thirteen-metre fishing schooner *Three Sisters* left its home port of Gaspé bound for Halifax. The owner, Edward Jordan, was desperate to sell enough fish to pay back the money he had borrowed to build his ship. Jordan was very proud of his schooner, which he had lovingly built himself and named for his three daughters. On board was a small crew, his wife Margaret, and their children. On arrival in Halifax, the men who loaned him the money took control of the ship when Jordan couldn't pay them immediately. Captain John Stairs was put in charge of the vessel and they set off for the Gaspé to get more fish. Jordan was so outraged at losing control of his ship that he began to plot his revenge.

Jordan was so frantic to get his ship back that when Captain Stairs went below deck to consult a chart, Jordan shot at him. The bullet grazed the captain before

What is a gibbet?

A gibbet is an iron, cage-like structure where the body of a pirate was hung as a warning to others. In the age of piracy, you could find a gibbet at the Narrows in St. John's, Newfoundland, and in three locations in Halifax: at Point Pleasant Park, on Georges Island, and on McNabs Island. The body of Edward Jordan was left on display for many years in a gibbet in Point Pleasant Park. If you visit the Maritime Museum of the Atlantic in Halifax you can see this model of a gibbet.

There be Pirates!

it hit another crew member in the chest, killing him. Stairs raced up to the deck, where Jordan had killed a second crew member. Despite his injuries, Captain Stairs managed to wrestle the weapon from Edward Jordan. Margaret saw what was going on and came to her husband's aid by attacking Stairs with a boat hook. To escape the violent couple, Stairs jumped overboard. Margaret and Edward Jordan pointed their ship towards Newfoundland, certain that Stairs wouldn't last long in the cold North Atlantic.

Amazingly, Captain Stairs was rescued. He reported Edward and Margaret Jordan to the British authorities, who offered a reward to anyone who could capture the husband and wife. As the *Three Sisters* was leaving Newfoundland bound for Ireland it was overtaken, and the couple was arrested and returned to Halifax to stand trial for piracy.

Was Margaret Jordan a vicious pirate intent on killing Captain Stairs? Or was she just trying to defend her husband? In some reports she was pardoned, since she did not actually kill anyone, and was freed to look after her children. In other versions of the story, she was hanged next to her husband. Edward Jordan was hanged on November 23, 1809, near where Halifax's Pier 21 Immigration Museum stands today.

Tools of the Trade

Write Like a Pirate—Make a Quill

Difficulty level: easy

Pirates who were able to read usually had the important job of navigating the ship to the next destination. A **quill** was used for writing, as the pen had yet to be invented. Follow these steps to make a quill from a drinking straw and scrap paper.

Supplies: drinking straw, glossy scrap paper, glue stick, scissors, soy sauce or balsamic vinegar

1. Use scissors to make a diagonal cut removing about 1cm of the end of the straw or feather.

2. Next, round off the tip by cutting off a small bit at the end.

3. Cut a vertical slit into the end, about 5mm long.

4. You can make the straw look like a feather by gluing the straw to the centre of a piece of paper, making sure the straw sticks out about 2-3cm from the bottom of the paper.

5. Glue the paper together, folding it so the straw is in the centre. Let dry and then cut out the shape of a feather. Cut slits down the paper to resemble a feather.

6. For ink, pour a small amount of balsamic vinegar or soy sauce into a container. Dip the tip of your quill into the ink and gently press the tip of the quill to your paper.

It will take practice and you will need to keep dipping the quill into the ink after making just one or two letters. Imagine how long it would have taken William Dampier to write several books using a quill and not a computer!

There be Pirates!

CHAPTER 5

Treasure

Clothes, food, rope, weapons, cargo, medicine, and a frying pan are just a few of the things that pirates stole. Pirate ships were often at sea for long periods of time and running out of food, drink, and supplies was a very real concern. It's not like a pirate ship in the middle of the North Atlantic could order supplies online, they had to get them from other ships or sail to a port to buy or steal them. If a merchant captain encountered a ship with a black flag, there was a chance that everyone on board his ship would die if they put up a fight. It was way better to surrender without a fight and give the pirates their cargo, if it meant that they would be left alive with the ship intact. But pirates were unpredictable. There is a record of pirates boarding a ship in the Caribbean and stealing only hats. A passenger on the ship recorded in his journal that the pirates said they got drunk the night before and everyone threw their hats overboard. Not even a pirate wanted to spend the day in the hot sun without a hat!

PORT ROYAL, PIRATE HAVEN

Located on the island of Jamaica in the middle of the Caribbean Sea, Port Royal was the largest English settlement in the New World and the centre of all trade during the Golden Age of Piracy. The harbour could shelter five hundred ships, with room to spare for

What are Pieces of Eight?

These silver coins were worth eight Spanish reales and were used all over the world from the 1500s to 1800s. When made from gold, pirates called the coin a doubloon. In the Golden Age of Piracy, it would take an ordinary sailor nearly two months to earn the equivalent of one doubloon. A pirate could buy a mansion in London for 3,000 pieces of eight. Since Long John Silver's parrot in the book *Treasure Island* first squawked "Pieces of eight!" in 1883, people have associated this coin with pirates (see page 70 for more about *Treasure Island*).

There be Pirates!

repairs. Some historians said that there was more cash spent here than in the city of London, and that most of it was stolen from Spanish settlements and ships. What better place for a pirate to find some excitement after a long and dreary voyage across the Atlantic? In Port Royal, a pirate could spend all of his booty in the taverns, drinking and gambling. Before an earthquake and tidal wave destroyed most of the city and killed more than half of the people in 1692, Port Royal was known as the "Wickedest City on Earth."

PIRATES AND BURIED TREASURE

Did pirates really bury treasure? Yes and no. If you watch movies or read books about pirates you would certainly think that every pirate buried a chest that was filled to the brim with gold, pearls, and precious gems. But the real story is that the loot was divided among the pirate crew, and most pirates spent their share as soon as they got to port. Historians are in agreement that most pirates did NOT bury their treasure. But there are a few exceptions, and it is the exceptions that give people hope of finding buried pirate treasure.

This Howard Pyle painting shows William Kidd burying treasure.

Did the famous pirate Captain William Kidd (1645–1701) bury his treasure on Oak Island, off of Nova Scotia? It is true that Kidd once buried Spanish coins, rubies, diamonds, silver, and gold. In 1699, in one of the very few known cases of a pirate burying treasure, Kidd buried his booty on Gardiners Island, in New York state, because he thought he was about to be caught and charged with piracy. Knowing that his loot was safe, Kidd sailed to Boston to face the charges. By this time, other pirates were being given pardons if they turned themselves in and swore to

There be Pirates!

end their evil ways. Kidd wasn't so lucky. He was jailed, then shipped to London for a trial. During his trial, Kidd wrote letters saying that he was innocent and would lead people to where he hid his treasure if they would get him out of jail. Kidd was hanged in 1701 without telling anyone where he may have hidden the rest of his loot. Many people hope that the treasure of William Kidd is still waiting to be found on Oak Island, or somewhere else in Atlantic Canada.

PIRATE TREASURE MAPS

Tiny Isle Haute, at the tip of the Bay of Fundy, has been the location of a few treasure hunts in the last hundred years. The Bay of Fundy is known for its thick fog and for having the highest tides in the world. Isle Haute has rock cliffs that rise ninety metres from the sea, making it almost inaccessible. Could there be a better place for a pirate to hide his treasure? Treasure hunters spent time here in 1925 and 1929 but no one knows if they found anything. There were rumours that jewels and gold were found and taken from beneath Isle Haute's rocky soil.

In 1952, with a map that was supposed to show the location of treasure buried by pirate Edward Low (see page 36), writer and adventurer Edward Snow headed to Isle Haute. Snow dug where the treasure map indicated and, with the use of a metal detector, found pieces of chain and other metal bits. He unearthed a human skull, more bones, and several old gold and silver coins. Was this the remains of a dead pirate left to keep others away from a huge treasure? Further digging turned up a few more coins, but the metal detector indicated that there was no more metal under the earth so Snow stopped his search. Did the earlier treasure hunters find a treasure chest and leave these few coins behind? We are all left to wonder if Isle Haute was the hiding place for the treasure of Edward Low, and if there might be more treasure waiting to be found on this tiny island in the Bay of Fundy.

TREASURE FOUND!

For nearly three hundred years, the wreck of the pirate ship *Whydah* sat undiscovered in shallow water off the New England coast near Cape Cod. Many people believed that this shipwreck was guarded by the ghost of its captain,

"Black Sam" Bellamy. The ship was caught in a vicious storm on April 23, 1717, hit an offshore sandbank, and broke apart. More than one hundred and forty pirates drowned but two pirates managed to survive and get to shore.

After many unsuccessful searches, the ship was discovered in 1984, buried under sand in water that was about six metres deep. More than 200,000 items have been recovered from the sunken ship, including 8,357 silver coins, 9 gold coins, 17 gold bars, and 14 gold nuggets. In addition to this treasure, searchers have found dishes, clothing, an ornate pistol with a length of silk ribbon still attached to its handle (just as you'd imagine hanging from Bartholomew Roberts's shoulder), navigational equipment, grenades, cannons, and cannonballs. The most intriguing piece was discovered in 2005 when searchers located what may be a wooden chest. Based on the stories of the only two surviving pirates, it is thought that the chest contains more coins, gold, and jewels. Unfortunately, divers haven't managed to free the chest and bring it to the surface to see what might be inside!

The Youngest Pirate

Searchers recovered a shoe, stocking, and leg bone from the wreck of the *Whydah*. Tests proved that the bone was from a child between eight and eleven years old and it is assumed to be that of John King. John became a pirate when the ship he was a passenger on was captured by Bellamy and his crew. Many historians believe that, at age eleven, John King was the youngest known pirate.

ANNE BONNY (APPROX. 1697–?) AND MARY READ (?–1720)

Why are Anne Bonny and Mary Read mentioned in almost every book about pirates? They weren't the only female pirates, but they were the only women included in *A General History of the Pyrates.*

Anne Bonny and Mary Read, from *A General History of the Pyrates.*

Anne Bonny was born in Ireland around 1697. She moved to America, where she eventually met and married her first husband. They then moved to the

Bahamas, where Anne met and fell in love with the dashing pirate Calico Jack Rackham. Anne wanted to stay with Rackham, but since women weren't allowed on pirate ships, she dressed in men's clothes and tricked almost everyone into thinking she was a man. Anne was a good sailor and skilled fighter and was as much of a pirate as any man on the ship.

Mary Read was born in England. She got married, but her husband died early in their marriage. With few other options, Mary dressed as a man and became a sailor. When her ship was captured by pirates, Mary ended up on Calico Jack's ship and also became a pirate.

While on Calico Jack's pirate ship, Anne and Mary were known for their bravery and fierceness when attacking other ships. They pulled their weight on the ship and did everything that the other pirates did. But pirate ships are small and, while it may have been easy to trick the rest of the men on board, Anne and Mary learned the truth about each other. One day, Calico Jack found Mary and Anne together and, fearing that he was going to lose his girlfriend to another man, Jack was ready to fight. To keep things from getting out of hand, Mary revealed herself to Jack. Surprise! Now there were two women dressed as men on the ship! An interesting turn of events for Jack, as he was the only man (on a ship full of pirates) who knew two of his crew were actually women. The trio kept the secret for a while and carried on as usual. Unfortunately for them, and everyone else on the ship, the pirates were captured by a pirate-hunter and all charged with piracy. At their trial, all of the men were found guilty and executed. Calico Jack Rackham's body was left in a gibbet not far from Port Royal, Jamaica.

> *"Had you fought like a man, you need not have been hung like a dog."*
>
> —ANNE BONNY TO JACK RACKHAM BEFORE HE WAS HUNG

Captain Kidd, Not Such a Bad Guy?

Some historians say that, compared to most pirates, Kidd wasn't so bad. Once Kidd and his crew needed help to fix their ship as all of their masts had been broken in a storm. The pirates made it to shore somewhere in Atlantic Canada and took shelter in a small fishing village. After the pirates promised not to hurt anyone, the locals gave them what was needed to fix the ship. When the work was finally done, Captain Kidd told the locals that he wanted to pay them for their supplies. The locals knew that any valuables this pirate had would be stolen, so they refused to take any money to avoid the bad luck that would follow. The story ends with Kidd sailing away and dropping gold and silver bars into the harbour as payment. Given how the locals felt about the pirates, the gold may still be there!

There was a different ending for Mary and Anne. While the trial proved that they were pirates and as guilty as the men in the crew, they weren't hanged. Both women were pregnant and therefore escaped the noose. Shortly after the trial Mary became ill and died in prison in 1720. There is no record of what happened to Anne Bonny or her baby.

MARIA LINDSEY, CANADA'S PIRATE QUEEN? (ACTIVE 1720–1740)

Was Maria Lindsey a bloodthirsty pirate who preyed on ships in Atlantic Canada between 1720 and 1740? Or were the stories about her and her husband, Eric Cobham, made up? From their base in Sandy Point, not far from present day Stephenville, Newfoundland, they raided ships travelling between what are now the Atlantic provinces. Once they captured a ship, they killed the crew, sunk the ship, and sold the cargo for a quick profit. Since the ships were never seen again, it was assumed that they were lost at sea.

Maria had a reputation for violence. Poison, stabbings, using sailors for target practice, and sewing live victims into a sack before throwing them overboard were ways that Maria is said to have tortured and killed her victims. Once the couple had made their fortune, they moved to France, bought an estate, had three children, and lived in luxury, so life should have been good. But Eric spent time with other women and Maria did not adjust to normal life on land and suffered a violent death. Her body was found at the base of a cliff. It is not known if she fell, jumped, or was pushed, but a doctor confirmed that she had taken, or been given, a large dose of a powerful drug shortly before her death.

Pirate Treasure on Oak Island?

People have been hunting for pirate treasure on Oak Island since 1795. Located about an hour's drive from Halifax, Nova Scotia, this little island may be hiding a vast treasure buried in a spot called the Money Pit. According to legend, three young men found a dip in the ground under the branch of an oak tree. A **block and tackle** was hanging from the branch. To them, this was proof that pirates had dug a hole and buried their treasure here. This discovery started a treasure hunt that has been going on for well over two hundred years. The truth is that no one knows what is buried there, but many people have spent the equivalent of a pirate's fortune trying to solve this mystery.

Explore Oak Island display in Chester, Nova Scotia.

There be Pirates!

The fact that Maria and Eric ruled the waters of Atlantic Canada for twenty years without ever being caught seems too incredible for some historians. Without any official records, they say, the stories about this violent duo are just stories. How do we have this much information about something that may have happened three hundred years ago? On his deathbed Eric confessed to a priest about his pirate past and his story was made into a book. His children were so shocked to learn about their parents' past that they tried to destroy every copy of the book. At least one copy was missed and is said to exist in an archive in France. Or is this is really just a rollicking, made-up story about Canada's Pirate Queen?

Spend like a Pirate—Make Some Pirate Coins

Difficulty level: easy
Supplies needed: clay, table knife, toothpick, paints, and paintbrush

To make some pirate coins, you need clay that air-dries or can be hardened in an oven. If you can't find any, search for a salt dough recipe and mix up a small batch.

Treasure

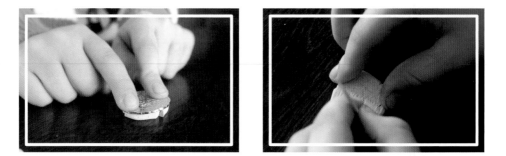

1. Roll several small clumps of clay into a ball, then flatten into circles. They don't have to be perfect, as old coins tend to be worn and uneven. Once you have the coins shaped the way you want them, it is time to decorate them.

2. Use a toothpick or a sharpened pencil to add numbers, letters, dots, shapes, or whatever you think looks great. Try pressing your coins on to surfaces with interesting textures to add dimension to your coins.

*You can also add very small bits of the clay to the surface of the coins to make raised shapes. Try adding crosses, crowns, or even a skull. Look at real coins for inspiration. If you don't like how they look, squish up the clay and start again!

3. When you have your coins looking the way that you want, get an adult to help you with the next part. Carefully follow the directions on the package or recipe to harden the clay. Some clay will dry if left out for a couple of days.

4. After your coins have hardened and are completely dry, you can paint them.

Once the paint dries, admire your own pirate booty then stash them in your pouch for safe keeping.

What did the pirate do before he buried his treasure?
Dug a hole!

CHAPTER 6
Pirate Legacy

Most of what we think we know about real pirates is based on fictionalized accounts of pirates from movies or books. Drawings by Howard Pyle, an artist in the late 1800s and early 1900s, served as the model for pirate costumes in movies and books. There are more than fifty movie versions of the book *Treasure Island*, even

Painting by Howard Pyle.

one that features the Muppets. *The Pirates of Penzance*, the opera by Gilbert and Sullivan first performed in 1879, was a funny look at fantasy pirates. The first movie in the *Pirates of the Caribbean* franchise was released in 2003, and was an instant success. The film series made LOTS of money—a few billion dollars! Pirates are a hugely popular source of entertainment for young and old.

PIRATE TALK AND TALK LIKE A PIRATE DAY

You have probably said "Arrr!" and "Ahoy, Matey" on September 19, Talk like a Pirate Day. What began as an inside joke between friends has grown into a silly celebration held all over the world. Even large corporations have joined in on the fun. Some restaurants give free food to anyone who talks like a pirate on September 19.

Aye, sounds like a good deal to me, matey!

Pirate Lingo

Here are some expressions to get you started talking like a pirate!

Ahoy - Hello
Aye - Yes
Aye, aye! – Yes, I'll do that right now!
Blow me down! – OH!!!
Heave ho! - Push or pull, hard!
Look lively! – Do it! or Get at it!
Pay no heed – Ignore this
Savvy? – Do you understand?
Shake a leg! – Look lively!
Show a leg! - Get out of bed!
Shiver me timbers! – Wow!

If you want more pirate lingo, check online for websites that will translate regular phrases into pirate talk. Savvy?

There be Pirates!

WHO WAS LONG JOHN SILVER?

Long John Silver is one of the best known pirates of all. You might even know what he looks like—tall, strong, with a handsome smile and winning personality. His most distinguishing feature was that he had only one leg but used a crutch so well that he moved around a ship almost as easily as any other sailor. The other thing you might know about this pirate was that he had a parrot named Captain Flint who was almost always on his shoulder. "Pieces of eight! Pieces of eight!" is what the parrot was always squawking, but it could say all sorts of other things too. You may even know that Long John Silver's parrot was nearly two hundred years old and that Silver had also known Bartholomew Roberts.

How do we know this much information about Long John Silver? Because he was the main character in the book *Treasure Island*, written by Robert Louis Stevenson and first published in 1883. This exciting tale of a race to find buried pirate treasure features a treasure map, a marooned sailor, a mutiny, trickery, betrayal, a black dot, lots of fighting, authentic dialogue, and accurate details about life on a ship. To create such a realistic story, the

Parrots and Pirates

Did pirates keep parrots as pets? Maybe. Did pirates have parrots on their shoulders while they were working? Probably not, as they would have gotten in the way of most jobs done on a ship. But during the age of piracy an exotic parrot could be used to bribe an official and was a popular souvenir. Many were brought back from the Caribbean to Europe where they could be sold for a large sum of money. When people dress up as pirates now they add a colourful parrot to their shoulder, just like that one-legged pirate, Long John Silver, in *Treasure Island*.

author did a great deal of research and is known to have consulted Charles Johnson's book (see page 10).

Treasure Island was popular from the moment it was published and has been in print for more than 130 years. The book has been made into dozens of movies and plays and is the inspiration for many of the images of pirates in books and movies. Without even realizing it, the story has probably influenced what you imagine pirates were like. When you hear a pirate say "Fifteen men on the Dead Man's Chest—Yo-ho-ho, and a bottle of rum!" you can give credit to the imagination of Robert Louis Stevenson and his book *Treasure Island*.

CAPTAIN HOOK

Captain Hook was a character in the play *Peter Pan, or, the Boy Who Wouldn't Grow Up*, written by J. M. Barrie and first performed in London in 1904. In 1911 Barrie published the novel *Peter and Wendy*, based on the play. Barrie said that he based Captain Hook's appearance on Blackbeard and that Hook's previous job was working as Blackbeard's bosun. Captain Hook was Peter Pan's arch-enemy and—you know this part—he had a hook for a

Tattoos

When you think of a pirate, chances are that you imagine someone with a large gold hoop in one ear and an impressive sleeve of tattoos. Pirates did NOT have tattoos until long after the Golden Age of Piracy. When Captain James Cook visited the Pacific islands in the late 1700s, he and his crew learned about the art of tattoos from the people of the South Pacific. Tattoos quickly became popular with sailors, then with the criminals who lived in port cities, and now with people of all ages and backgrounds. Interestingly, some sailors would get a tattoo of a swallow after sailing eight thousand kilometres. A swallow is a bird known for travelling great distances before returning home and for this reason, is also a popular name for ships.

71

hand because Peter Pan chopped his hand off and fed it to a crocodile. If you can describe exactly what Captain Hook looks like, you are likely thinking of the Disney cartoon version of the movie released in 1953.

JACK SPARROW

Jack Sparrow is the captain of the *Black Pearl* and is well known for being able to talk or trick his way out of almost any situation. He is played by Johnny Depp in the *Pirates of the Caribbean* movies. The creators say Jack Sparrow is a composite of many pirates. The movies are based on the attraction of the same name

List of Most Successful Pirates

How successful were the pirates who sailed around Atlantic Canada? Pretty successful. *Forbes Magazine,* an American business journal, made a list of the top twenty most successful pirates ever and calculated what the value of their loot would be today. Here is how some of the pirates in this book measure up:

1. Samuel Bellamy	$120 million
5. Bartholomew Roberts	$32 million
10. Blackbeard	$12.5 million
14. Howell Davis	$4.5 million
18. Edward Low	$1.8 million
19. Calico Jack Rackham	$1.5 million

There be Pirates!

found at Disney theme parks. If you are going to dress up as a pirate for Halloween, chances are that you will be looking a lot like Jack Sparrow.

Dress like a Pirate—Make an Eye Patch

Difficulty level: medium

Supplies needed: 2 pieces of shoelace, string or ribbon (each about 50cm long), scrap paper, pencil, ruler, and a piece of felt at least 7cm by 7cm. You could use leather left from making your pouch, or even an old sock.

1. Using the ruler, measure the distance across your eyebrow, from the centre of your nose to the side of your face.

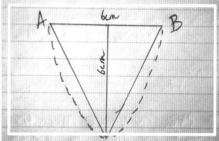

2. In the middle of your piece of scrap paper, draw a line this length and make an 'A' at one end and a 'B' at the other end.

3. Using the ruler, measure from the top of your eyebrow, at the middle of your eye, to the bottom of your cheekbone.

4. On your scrap paper, draw a line this length starting in the centre of the line, between 'A' and 'B.'

5. Draw a line connecting the 'A' to the bottom of the centre line, then draw another line to connect the 'B' to the bottom of centre line. Now you have an eye patch shape. If it seems too small, draw a line around the outside to make a bigger patch. If it is too big, draw a line around the inside.

6. To make a paper pattern, cut out on the lines that best fit your eye.

Hold the cut-out pattern up to your eye and check in a mirror to make sure that the shape covers your eye and looks piratey.

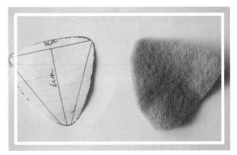

7. Lay the paper pattern on top of your piece of fabric, leather, or sock.

Cut out around the paper pattern to make your eye patch.

8. Carefully make small holes close to the edge of the fabric where the 'A' and 'B' were on the paper pattern. Put the end of one shoelace in one hole and tie. Tie the second shoelace into the second hole.

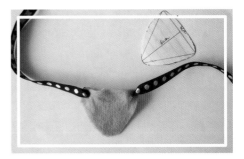

9. Position on your face so that the patch covers your eye and have someone tie a knot at the back of your head, so that your eye patch is comfortable and won't fall down.

Look in the mirror. ARRR! Who is that pirate?

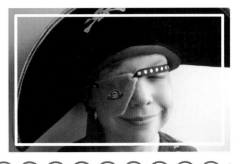

What is a pirate's favourite letter?
Arrrrr!

Pirates Today

"Piracy, the scourge of the seventeenth and eighteenth centuries, has emerged from the history books and has returned with deadly, terrifying results."
—Dangerous Waters: Modern Piracy and Terror on the High Seas by John S. Burnett

There are still pirates roaming the oceans of the world and pillaging ships of all sizes. Since many goods travel to their markets in ships, there are people stealing the cargo and making money by stopping these ships. Today, most pirates work in the waters off the poorest countries in the world. Piracy involves a few people in a speedboat boarding a large ship that may have a crew of only twelve people. These pirates steal the personal belongings of the crew, the cash from the safe, and easy-to-carry cargo. Other pirates kidnap the crew and demand huge sums of money for their release or steal the entire ship, sell all of the cargo, and then reuse the ship.

FIGHTING PIRACY TODAY

You can go online and look at a live piracy map made by the International Chamber of Commerce. There's also

Digital Piracy

The copying of digital content such as music, movies, software, and books is another form of theft that is sometimes called piracy. When people download a movie or song from a file sharing site without paying for it, the creators don't receive payment for their work. Rules about this vary from country to country and are changing as technology changes. And, just like real pirates, people find ways to work around the rules to get the digital content that they want. But it's a very real crime and can involve hefty fines or even jail time.

a twenty-four-hour hotline that sailors can call to hear reports about where there is a threat or to report piracy. Ship owners have developed ways to keep ships safe from pirates. The use of powerful water hoses, high-pitched noises that can seriously damage a person's hearing, loud alarms, and flashing lights will keep pirates away and warn others in the area. Some large cargo ships can activate an electric current on their railing to keep pirates from boarding. Smaller

There is safety in numbers when pleasure boats raft up, or anchor together.

There be Pirates!

ships and yachts are also a target for pirates, but sailors are sharing information and strategies to stay safe. With these measures in place, instances of piracy are decreasing. But chances are, just like you read at the beginning of this book, piracy will be around as long as there are ships.

CELEBRATING PIRATES

Pirate festivals and celebrations take place all over— in Harbour Grace, Newfoundland, in Liverpool, Nova Scotia, in Key West, Florida, and even in Toronto. If you can't participate in a pirate event, gather some friends and have your own pirate party. If that isn't your style, make a pirate craft, borrow a classic pirate movie from the library, or read a pirate book.

You can find this pirate ship at a playground in Liverpool, Nova Scotia.

WHY ARE WE STILL FASCINATED WITH PIRATES?

People of all ages love to dress up as pirates.

Pirates from the Golden Age of Piracy continue to interest people. We love movies and books about pirates and enjoy dressing up as a character from our favourite pirate movie. Pirates were violent criminals who could be compared to modern day terrorists or gang members. No one would want to celebrate a terrorist, yet we celebrate all things related to pirates. Why? Most of what we think we know about pirates is not real. Movies and books about pirates have taken some of the interesting and neat things about piracy, such as tropical beaches and a no-rules lifestyle, and downplayed the violent and criminal behaviour. As entertainment, pirate stories are fun, but they are stories. So, enjoy reading novels and watching pirate movies with the knowledge you now have and dazzle your friends with some real information about pirates!

There be Pirates!

Acknowledgements

Nick Barry is the best husband in the world. Without his support, help, and ideas, I'd never have been able to write this book. Thanks for watching all of those pirate movies!

Thanks to everyone who helped me, at every point along the way:

Alex and Hope Barry

Norma Hamilton

Jackie and Barry Hamilton

Captain John Warr

Lynn and Mike McShane

Ken Boehner

Alison, Andrew, Ainslie, and Oliver Stickings, enthusiastic crafters

Wendy Matheson of DaveShootsBookseller.com

Dr. Cheryl Fury, @TudorWench, professor of History, writer, and fellow pirate lover. Thanks for helping me, at the busiest time of the academic year, with your careful reading of my manuscript, offers of research material, and advice

Conception Bay Museum—staff and Board of Directors, especially Patrick Collins

Staff of Port Saint John

Staff of the New Brunswick Museum, especially Gary Hughes, Peter Larocque, and Jennifer Longon

Staff of Nimbus Publishing, especially Whitney Moran, Lexi Harrington, and Emily MacKinnon

I couldn't have completed this book without the support of all of my colleagues at the Saint John Free Public Library, the Fundy Library Region, and New Brunswick Public Library Service. Library staff found books, took photos, suggested movies, dressed as pirates, and helped me in more ways than they will ever know. THANKS, I am lucky to work with each and every one of you!

A special shout out to all of the other pirate lovers out there who write, sing, make movies, blog, tweet, and dream about the swashbucklers and rogues of the Atlantic.

Many people helped me as I worked on this book. If there are mistakes in this book, they are not responsible.

There be Pirates!

Glossary

Articles: The rules for sailors on a pirate ship.

Astrolabe: A navigational instrument used by sailors to calculate latitude, which is the distance of something from the equator, measured in degrees.

Barnacle: A sea creature related to crabs and lobsters that attaches to the bottom of a ship, or slang for a person who is difficult to get rid of.

Block and tackle: Rope and pully device used to lift heavy loads.

Boatswain: Ship's officer responsible for equipment, also called a bosun.

Booty: Stolen treasure.

Breeches: Pants that end just below the knee.

Careen: To tip a ship on its side, in order to clean or repair the bottom.

Compass: An instrument that indicates direction, when the needle points to the north.

Convoy: A group of ships travelling together.

Court-martialled: Convicted of an offence in a military court.

Cutlass: A short, curved sword.

Dry dock: A structure that can be emptied of water, for repairing the bottom of a ship.

Gaelic: The traditional languages spoken by the Celts in Ireland and Scotland.

Haven: A safe port.

Malnutrition: The result of having a poor diet.

Marooned: To be left on an island or beach.

Merchant ship: A ship that carries cargo, such as grain.

Mutiny: A revolt against authority figures, especially by sailors against their captains.

Navy: The ships and crew used to defend a country from its enemies.

Pardon: To forgive or excuse someone for committing a crime.

Pitch: A sticky substance that comes from the sap of a tree, used to waterproof wooden boats and barrels.

Pounds: The official currency of the United Kingdom.

Privateer: Refers to the ship itself, or the captain and crew of a private ship, with government permission to attack enemy ships during a time of war.

Provisions: Food, drink, and supplies needed for a journey.

Quartermaster: The second-in-command on a pirate ship, responsible for dividing loot and keeping the crew in order.

Quill: A pen made from a feather, the end of which is dipped in ink.

Salmagundi: A mixture of meat, eggs, and vegetables made into a stew or salad.

Schooner: A ship with at least two masts.

Telescope: A device used to bring distant objects into view.

Vessel: A ship used to carry people or cargo.

Recommended Reading

"I ransack public libraries, and find them full of sunken treasure."
—Virginia Woolf

NON-FICTION BOOKS FOR CHILDREN

Chrisp, Peter. *Pirates*. New York: Kingfisher, 2011.

Gilbert, Henry. *The Book of Pirates*. London: Bracken Books, 1986.

Hamilton, Libby. *Ultimate Pirate Handbook*. Somerville, Mass.: Templar Books, 2015.

Howard, Barnaby. *Best Book of Pirates*. New York: Kingfisher, 2002.

Jones, Rob Lloyd. *The Story of Pirates*. London: Usborne, 2007.

Malam, John. *You Wouldn't Want To Be This Pirate's Prisoner!* Toronto: Franklin Watts, 2002.

Martin, Silas. *Pirates*. Macmillan Children's Books, 1980.

Matthews, John. *Pirates*. New York: Atheneum, 2006.

Morris, Neil. *Pirates* (Amazing History series). Mankato, Mn.: Smart Apple Media, 2008.

O'Donnell, Liam. *Pirate Ships*. Mankato, Mn.: Capstone, 2007.

Piratepedia. Ed. by Alisha Niehaus. New York: DK Publishing, 2007.

Platt, Richard. *Eyewitness Guides: Pirate*. New York: DK Publishing, 2007.

Savery, Annabel. *It's Amazing! Pirates.* Mankato, Mn.: Smart Apple Media, 2013.

Steele, Phillip. *Pirates.* New York: Kingfisher, 1997.

Wright, Rachel. *Pirates: Facts, Things to Make, Activities.* Toronto: Franklin Watts, 1991.

PICTURE BOOKS

Gilman, Phoebe. *Grandma and the Pirates.* Toronto: Scholastic, 1990.

Gilman, Phoebe. *Pirate Pearl.* Toronto: North Winds, 1998.

Lawson, Julie. *The Pirates of Captain McKee.* Toronto: Scholastic, 2008.

Morgan, Allen. *Matthew and the Midnight Pirates.* Toronto: Stoddart, 1998.

JUNIOR NOVELS

Bailey, Linda. *Seven Dead Pirates.* Toronto: Tundra, 2015.

Chantler, Scott. *Pirates of the Silver Coast.* Toronto: Kids Can Press, 2014.

Fagan, Cary. *Jacob Two-Two on the High Seas.* Toronto: Tundra Books, 2009.

Inglis, Kate. *The Dread Crew: Flight of the Griffons.* Halifax: Nimbus, 2014.

Inglis, Kate. *The Dread Crew: Pirates of the Backwoods.* Halifax: Nimbus, 2010.

There be Pirates!

Johansen, K.V. *Torrie and the Pirate Queen.* Toronto: Annick, 2005.

Lawrence, Iain. *The Buccaneers.* New York: Delacorte Press, 2001.

NON-FICTION BOOKS FOR ADULTS

Botting, Douglas. *The Pirates.* Alexandra, Virginia: Time-Life Books, 1978.

Burnett, John S. *Dangerous Waters: Modern Piracy and Terror on the High Seas.* New York: Dutton, 2002.

Carni, Marco and Flora, Macallun. *Pirates: A Swashbuckling Journey Across the Seven Seas.* Bath, UK.: Paragon Publishing.

Conlin, Dan. *Pirates of the Atlantic: Robbery, Murder and Mayhem off the Canadian East Coast.* Halifax: Formac, 2009.

Cordingly, David. *Under the black flag: the romance and reality of life among the pirates.* New York: Harcourt Brace & Co., 1995.

Crooker, William S. *Pirates of the North Atlantic.* Halifax: Nimbus, 2004.

Crooker, William S. *Tracking Treasure: In search of East Coast Bounty.* Halifax: Nimbus, 1998.

Earle, Peter. *The Pirate Wars.* New York: Thomas Dunne Books, 2003.

Fury, Cheryl A. *Tides in the Affairs of Men: The Social History of Elizabethan Seamen, 1580-1603.* Westport, Connecticut: Greenwood Press, 2002.

Fury, Cheryl A. *The social history of English seamen 1485-1649.* Rochester, NY.: Boydell Press, 2012.

Fury, Cheryl A. *The social history of English seamen 1650-1815.* Rochester, NY.: Boydell Press, 2017.

Horwood, Harold and Ed Butts. *Pirates and Outlaws of Canada, 1610-1932.* Toronto: Doubleday, 1984.

Horwood, Harold. *Plunder and Pillage: Atlantic Canada's Brutal & Bloodthirsty Pirates and Privateers.* Halifax: Formac, 2011.

Little, Benerson. *How History's Greatest Pirates Pillaged, Plundered and Got Away With It.* Beverly, MA.: Fair Winds Press, 2011.

Marsters, Roger. *Bold Privateers: Terror, Plunder and Profit on Canada's Atlantic Coast.* Halifax: Formac, 2004.

Pirates: *Terror on the High Seas – from the Caribbean to the South China Sea.* Consulting editor: David Cordingly. East Bridgewater, MA.: World Publications Group, 2007.

Rediker, Marcus. *Between the Devil and the Deep Blue Sea.* New York: Cambridge University Press, 1999.

Rediker, Marcus. *Outlaws of the Atlantic: Sailors, Pirates, and Motley Crews in the Age of Sail.* Boston: Beacon Press, 2014.

Rediker, Marcus. *Villains of all Nations: Atlantic Pirates in the Golden Age.* Boston: Beacon Press, 2014.

There be Pirates!

Image Credits

Andrew Stickings: 31, 32, 41, 42, 65, 66, 73, 74

Bridgeman Images: 42, 60

Can Stock: 7, 20, 21, 34, 35, 48, 53, 59

Danny Hennigar, curator, Explore Oak Island Display, Chester, Nova Scotia: 64

Emily King: 46

Howard Pyle paintings courtesy of Bridgeman Images: 22, 56, 67

Joann Hamilton-Barry: 38, 41, 52, 77

Ken Boehner: vi, 36, 50, 70

Lynn Hamilton McShane: 13

New Brunswick Museum: 11, 43, 44

Nova Scotia Archives: 40

Patricia Hamilton-Warr: 76

Paul Boehner: i, 5, 25

Saint John Free Public Library: 78

Index

There be Pirates!

OTHER BOOKS IN THE COMPASS: TRUE STORIES FOR KIDS SERIES

Children of the Titanic
ISBN: 978-155109-892-0

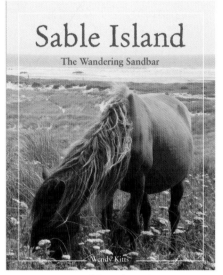

Sable Island
ISBN: 978-155109-865-4

Birchtown
ISBN: 978-177108-166-5

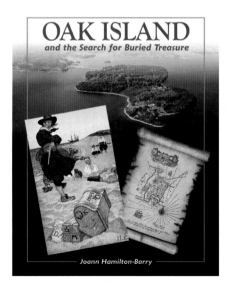

Oak Island
ISBN: 978-177108-342-3